fab fast food!

hamlyn

fab fast food!

Sunil Vijayakar

First published in the U.K. in 1999
by Hamlyn, a division of
Octopus Publishing Group Ltd
2–4 Heron Quays
London E14 4JP

ISBN 0 600 60468 3

Printed in Great Britain

NOTES

Both metric and imperial measurements have been given in all
recipes. Use one set of measurements only and not a
mixture of both.

Standard level spoon measurements are used in all recipes.
1 tablespoon = one 15 ml spoon
1 teaspoon = one 5 ml spoon

Eggs should be medium to large unless otherwise stated.
The Department of Health advises that eggs should not be
consumed raw. This book contains dishes made with raw or
lightly cooked eggs. It is prudent for more vulnerable people
such as pregnant and nursing mothers, invalids, the elderly,
babies and young children to avoid uncooked or lightly cooked
dishes made with eggs. Once prepared, these dishes should
be kept refrigerated and used promptly.

Milk should be full fat unless otherwise stated.

Poultry should be cooked thoroughly. To test if poultry is cooked,
pierce the flesh through the thickest part with a skewer or fork –
the juices should run clear, never pink or red.

Do not re-freeze a dish that has been frozen previously.

Pepper should be freshly ground black pepper unless
otherwise stated.

Fresh herbs should be used, unless otherwise stated. If
unavailable, use dried herbs as an alternative but halve the
quantities stated.

Measurements for canned food have been given as a standard
metric equivalent.

Nuts and nut derivatives
This book includes dishes made with nuts and nut derivatives.
It is advisable for customers with known allergic reactions to
nuts and nut derivatives and those who may be potentially
vulnerable to these allergies, such as pregnant and nursing
mothers, invalids, the elderly, babies and children, to avoid
dishes made with nuts and nut oils. It is also prudent to check
the labels of pre-prepared ingredients for the possible inclusion
of nut derivatives.

Ovens should be preheated to the specified temperature – if
using a fan-assisted oven, follow the manufacturer's
instructions for adjusting the time and the temperature.

Contents

Introduction

Despite their hectic life styles, many people are now rejecting processed foods and frozen meals, instead turning once again to quality and flavour. People expect more from their food than they did just a few years ago, and home cooking is very much in vogue again. But time constraints mean that the modern cook has to produce a delicious and nutritious meal in next to no time. This is quite a tall order and many people turn to pasta night after night because it is convenient, healthy and filling. There are other options for home-cooked meals, however, and *Fab Fast Food!* shows you how to create a wide range of dishes, easily encompassing styles from all over world, in about 30 minutes or less, using widely accessible ingredients.

As well as being convenient, quick cooking is actually the best way to treat many fresh ingredients, such as fish and seafood, crisp vegetables, juicy fruit and tender cuts of meat. These foods are at their best when cooked only for a short time as they retain their texture and flavour, and also their nutrients. In fact, many of the popular cooking trends today are very fast and simple, including stir-frying, grilling and griddling, and utilize quality ingredients cooked lightly to stay fresh and naturally delicious.

Main-meal salads are also popular and are perfect for the busy cook. Great salad ingredients are readily available, and many are sold ready prepared. This book includes recipes for many fantastic hot and cold salads, including Grilled Aubergine and Courgette Salad with Honey-mint Dressing (see page 28) and Panzanella (see page 32), but salads are versatile and can be made from whatever you have to hand. Choose from a selection of chopped raw vegetables such as salad leaves, cucumber, tomatoes, avocado, celery, carrot, bean sprouts, cabbage, onions, mushrooms and fresh herbs. Include a selection of steamed, grilled or griddled vegetables such as new potatoes, asparagus, baby courgettes, mixed peppers, aubergines and fennel. Perhaps throw

in some cooked meats or fish such as mussels, tuna or anchovies. Nuts, fruits and cheeses also make welcome additions. Simply toss your chosen ingredients with one of the dressings on page 9 and serve with crusty bread.

SHOPPING

The key to *Fab Fast Food!* is regular shopping to make sure you have a good selection of ingredients from which to make a quick meal. Some convenience foods are well worth having and involve little preparation.

STORECUPBOARD ITEMS

Many canned or dried foods are invaluable as stand-bys in the store-cupboard, allowing you to produce varied and interesting meals at the drop of a hat. Some vegetables lend themselves to being preserved in oil or canned; the following items are useful additions to pasta sauces, salads and risotto: olives, tomatoes, sun-dried tomatoes, pimentoes and roasted peppers, capers and caperberries, bamboo shoots and artichoke hearts.

Canned pulses such as chickpeas and beans are also perfect for quick meals as they are already cooked and make fine additions to salads (see page 34), couscous dishes (see page 32), curries and stir-fries.

Cans or jars of fish are also great ingredients which take up little space in the cupboard but impart wonderful flavours to many dishes. Choose from tuna, crab meat, anchovies, mussels, clams, baby squid and octopus, and smoked oysters or mussels. The latter will add a delicious smoky flavour to tomato-based pasta sauces and risotto, or can be tossed with cooked spaghetti, fried grated courgette and Parmesan shavings for a simple, sophisticated supper.

Pasta and noodles are the ultimate in convenience foods. Dried varieties last a long time, while fresh ones can be frozen successfully. Rice is also essential. Keep basmati for pilaffs and as a simple accompaniment to quick curries and stir-fries, and arborio for risotto. Brown rice is also useful to have for salads. It can be cooked a day in advance, while you are preparing the previous evening's meal, for use cold the next day in a salad. Couscous and

bulgar wheat are both quick to prepare and make interesting meals.

A few basic oils and vinegars can make a host of varied dressings for salads and pasta dishes and are also great for drizzling over plain meats and vegetables. Stock extra virgin olive oil for salads and pasta; a lighter olive oil for cooking; walnut, hazelnut and sesame oils for dressing salads and steamed vegetables; red and white wine vinegar for salads; and balsamic vinegar for salads and for dressing cooked foods. It is best to store oils out of direct sunlight to retain their flavour for longer.

Spices make a big difference to foods, transforming just a few basic ingredients into an interesting meal. Keep the following in the kitchen: ground cumin, coriander, turmeric, curry powder or paste, sesame seeds, chilli powder, cayenne, sea salt and black peppercorns. Soy sauce, Thai fish sauce, mustards, honey and coconut milk are all things that keep for a long time and can be used to pep up salads and savoury dishes.

FRESH INGREDIENTS
Milk, butter, cream or crème fraîche and yogurt will all stay fresh in the refrigerator for many days and can be used in a variety of sweet and savoury dishes. Cheeses such as Parmesan, Cheddar and mozzarella are good in salads, pasta dishes, risotto and pizzas. Haloumi and feta both have very long best-before dates, making them useful to keep for versatile last minute creations.

Most people stock a selection of fresh vegetables and fruits, but the following are particularly useful to have to hand. Fresh ginger, garlic and onions (both red and white) are used in countless dishes and are absolute essentials. Salad leaves don't keep for long, but mixed bags of ready-washed leaves are especially convenient.

Tomatoes are very versatile with heaps of flavour for quick sauces, salads and salsas. Courgettes can be used in many similar ways, both raw and briefly cooked.

FROZEN STAND-BYS

The freezer is an important extension of the storecupboard and offers many time-saving possibilities. Vegetables freeze well and many can be cooked from frozen, such as peas, spinach and sweetcorn. Frozen cooked prawns or raw tiger prawns are also invaluable for salads, sauces, stir-fries and curries.

Part-baked breads such as rolls, ciabatta and French sticks can be cooked from frozen to accompany soups and salads to complete a meal. Frozen pastries like shortcrust, puff and filo make instant pies and tarts in a fraction of the time it would take you to make your own. Ice creams and sorbets and frozen berries make a great base for quick desserts.

TIME-SAVING TIPS

Often most of the time it takes to make a meal is spent preparing the ingredients, so it makes sense to buy ready-washed and even chopped vegetables for instant stir-fries and salads. Likewise, buy fish filleted and meat boned or cubed, if possible.

When time is limited, the key to successful and enjoyable cooking is advance planning. Plan what you are going to cook the day before so that you can check you have the necessary ingredients and have time to defrost frozen ones. Get into the habit of doing this while you are cooking dinner each night so that you are always a day ahead. When you come home the next day to cook the meal, you can start cooking straight away.

Another good tip is to prepare all the ingredients before you start to cook; form a sort of assembly line, arranging them in the order that they will be needed, to speed up the cooking process.

Make double or triple batches of basic dishes such as pasta sauces, pestos, stocks, salad dressings and risotto and freeze the leftovers or store in the refrigerator for a quick meal next time.

FLAVOUR OF THE MONTH

You can easily prepare one of the luxurious recipes on page 9 and use them as alternatives to the suggested butters or dressings within this book or to add something special to one of your own favourite recipes.

FLAVOURED OILS

Flavoured oils such as rosemary, chilli, basil, lemon and garlic are perfect for drizzling over cooked fish, meat or vegetables and salads. To make a flavoured oil, gently warm some light olive oil in a saucepan with the chosen ingredient: herbs, garlic, chillies or strips of lemon rind, pricked all over to release their aroma. Remove from the heat and allow the mixture to infuse as it cools. Pour into a dry sterilised bottle and store in the refrigerator.

FLAVOURED BUTTERS

The butter melts into the food and imparts the flavour of the ingredients mixed with it. When making a butter, make more than you need and freeze some to be used later from frozen.

Spicy Butter

125 g (4 oz) butter, softened
1 teaspoon ground ginger
1 teaspoon chilli powder
½ teaspoon cumin seeds
2 teaspoons chopped fresh coriander

Mix the ingredients together in a bowl. Turn the butter out on to a large piece of clingfilm and press it out into a sausage shape. Wrap the clingfilm around the butter and twist the ends. Store in the refrigerator or freezer. Slice off portions as required.

Rosemary and Garlic Butter

125 g (4 oz) butter, softened
1 teaspoon crushed garlic
1 teaspoon freshly-ground black
    pepper
2 tablespoons chopped rosemary
    leaves

Follow the method above.

Orange and Parsley Butter

125 g (4 oz) butter, softened
1 tablespoon orange juice
2 teaspoons finely grated orange rind
2 teaspoons finely chopped parsley

Follow the method above.

Japanese-style Butter

125 g (4 oz) butter, softened
1 teaspoon sesame seeds
1 tablespoon prepared wasabi paste
1 tablespoon dark soy sauce

Follow the method above.

Salad dressings

A good dressing will transform a few raw ingredients into a memorable meal. Experiment and adapt these to include your favourite ingredients.

Quick Basic Dressing

3 tablespoons extra virgin olive oil
1 tablespoon balsamic vinegar
1 teaspoon honey
1 garlic clove, crushed
salt and pepper

Place all the ingredients in a screw-top jar and shake to blend thoroughly. Pour over prepared salad leaves.

Mint and Honey Dressing

5 tablespoons extra virgin olive oil
2 tablespoons finely chopped mint
2 tablespoons lime juice
2 tablespoons honey
salt and pepper

Follow the method above.

Herb and Tomato Mayonnaise

4–5 tablespoons mayonnaise
1 tablespoon sun-dried tomato paste
1 tablespoon mustard
2 tablespoons chopped mixed herbs
1 tablespoon lemon juice
salt and pepper

Put all the ingredients into a small bowl and mix well to blend.
Toss with hot potatoes or steamed green beans, if liked.

Quick Lemon and Honey Yogurt Dressing

200 ml (7 fl oz) plain yogurt
1 tablespoon lemon juice
2 teaspoons honey
1 tablespoon chopped parsley
salt and pepper

Mix all the ingredients together in a small bowl, then chill for at least *10 minutes* before serving.
This dressing is perfect for spooning over steamed sprouts, cucumber or crunchy fresh greens.

Starters and Snacks

The following recipes are very deceptive. They look exquisite and complicated, but in fact, couldn't be easier to prepare. Some of the dishes do not even require cooking, making them ideal for impromptu entertaining.

Tomato, Oregano and Mozzarella Tartlets

250 g (8 oz) puff pastry
6 tablespoons sun-dried
   tomato paste
3 plum tomatoes, deseeded
   and coarsely chopped
125 g (4 oz) mozzarella
   cheese, coarsely diced
8 black olives, pitted and
   coarsely chopped

1 garlic clove, finely chopped
2 tablespoons coarsely
   chopped oregano
1 tablespoon pine nuts
a little olive oil
salt and pepper
mixed salad leaves, to serve

1 Line a large baking sheet with nonstick baking paper. Roll out the pastry on a lightly floured board to 3 mm (⅛ inch) thick. Use a large round cutter to stamp out 6 x 12 cm (5 inch) circles and place them on the prepared baking sheet.

2 Spread 1 tablespoon sun-dried tomato paste over each pastry circle. In a small bowl, mix the tomatoes, mozzarella, olives, garlic, oregano and pine nuts, and season well. Divide this mixture between the pastry circles.

3 Drizzle a little olive oil over the tartlets and bake them in a preheated oven, 200°C (400°F), Gas Mark 6, for *20 minutes* or until the pastry is golden. Serve at once with mixed salad leaves.

Preparation time: 15 minutes
Cooking time: about 20 minutes
Serves 6

Cook's Tip
Puff pastry is the richest of all pastries, and it involves quite a long process to make it from scratch. Therefore, it is really convenient to buy it ready-made and some pastry even comes ready-rolled. It is best to use the pastry slightly chilled in order to achieve a light, flaky texture.

Potato Cakes with Trout Caviar and Coriander Cream

400 g (13 oz) potatoes, grated
1 egg, beaten
2 teaspoons coarse-grain or
   Dijon mustard
4 spring onions, finely
   chopped
1 tablespoon vegetable oil

125 g (4 oz) crème fraîche
4 tablespoons finely chopped
   coriander leaves
50 g (2 oz) trout or salmon
   caviar
salt and pepper
coriander leaves, to garnish

1 Squeeze out any moisture from the grated potatoes and place them in a bowl. Add the egg, mustard and spring onions. Season well to taste and mix thoroughly.

2 Heat the oil in a large nonstick frying pan over a medium heat. Drop 8 mounds of potato mixture into the pan and press each one down with the back of the spoon to make a 5 mm (¼ inch) thick cake. Fry for *2–3 minutes* on each side, until pale golden, then drain well on kitchen paper. (If you do not have a large frying pan, cook the mixture in 2 batches and keep the first batch hot while cooking the second.)

3 Mix the crème fraîche and the chopped coriander, and add seasoning to taste. Top each potato cake with a little coriander cream and add a little trout or salmon caviar. Garnish with coriander leaves and serve hot.

Preparation time: 10 minutes
Cooking time: 4–6 minutes
Serves 4

Cook's Tip
Trout caviar is slightly smaller in size and often less expensive. If you are feeling really extravagant, try some Beluga caviar.

Strawberry and Cucumber Salad with a Balsamic Dressing

Some people may find this combination a little peculiar, but dressing strawberries with balsamic vinegar or a sprinkling of black pepper brings out their flavour.

1 large cucumber, halved
   lengthways, deseeded and
   thinly sliced
250 g (8 oz) strawberries,
   halved or quartered if large

BALSAMIC DRESSING:
1 tablespoon balsamic vinegar
1 teaspoon coarse-grain
   mustard
1 teaspoon clear honey
3 tablespoons olive oil
salt and pepper

← TOO OILY FOR KB

1 Place the cucumber and strawberries in a shallow bowl.

2 To make the dressing, put all the ingredients in a screw-top jar and shake well.

3 Taste the dressing for seasoning and adjust if necessary before pouring it over the cucumber and strawberries. Toss lightly and chill for *5–10 minutes* before serving.

Preparation time: 10 minutes, plus chilling
Serves 4–6

Smoked Duck and Mango Salad

200 g (7 oz) smoked duck
   breast, thinly sliced
2 small ripe mangoes, peeled,
   stoned and thinly sliced
2 tablespoons pomegranate
   seeds or redcurrants

CURRIED MAYONNAISE:
4 tablespoons mayonnaise
1 teaspoon mild curry paste
1 tablespoon lemon juice
salt and pepper
mint leaves, to garnish

1 Arrange the duck, mango and pomegranate seeds or redcurrants on 4 serving plates.

2 Mix the mayonnaise with the curry paste and lemon juice. Season the mayonnaise well and divide it among the 4 salads. Scatter mint leaves over the salads to garnish.

Preparation time: 10 minutes
Serves 4

Variation
Duck and fruit make a lovely combination. You could substitute the pomegranate or redcurrants with cranberries or cherries.

Thai Style Coconut Mussels

2 kg (4 lb) mussels
600 ml (1 pint) vegetable stock
400 ml (14 fl oz) coconut milk
grated rind and juice of
    2 limes
2 lemon grass stalks, lightly
    bruised
1 tablespoon green curry
    paste
3 red chillies, deseeded and
    finely sliced

4 tablespoons chopped
    coriander leaves
2 spring onions, shredded
salt and black pepper

GARNISH (OPTIONAL):
1 red chilli, deseeded and
    chopped
chopped coriander leaves

1 Scrub the mussels in cold water, scrape off any barnacles and
pull away the dark hairy beards that protrude from the shells.
Discard any broken shells or open mussels that do not close
when tapped sharply.

2 Pour the stock and coconut milk into a large saucepan and
bring to a boil. Stir in the lime rind and juice, lemon grass, curry
paste, chillies, coriander, spring onions and seasoning to taste.

3 Add the mussels, cover the pan and bring back to the boil.
Cook for *3–4 minutes* or until all the mussels have opened.
Discard any shells that remain closed. Use a slotted spoon to
divide the mussels among 4 individual serving bowls and keep
warm until ready to serve.

4 Bring the stock to a vigorous boil and boil hard for about
5 minutes to reduce it and concentrate the flavour. Strain the
stock through a fine sieve, then ladle it over the mussels.

5 Garnish the bowls of mussels with chopped red chilli, plenty
of chopped coriander leaves and the lemon grass, if liked. Serve
immediately while still hot.

Preparation time: 20 minutes
Cooking time: about 10 minutes
Serves 4

Mediterranean Bruschetta

1 yellow pepper, deseeded
    and cut lengthways into
    8 strips
1 red pepper, deseeded and
    cut lengthways into 8 strips
2 courgettes, sliced
    diagonally
1 red onion, sliced and
    separated into rings

4 tablespoons olive oil
2 garlic cloves, peeled but
    left whole
1 ciabatta loaf or baguette
1 small ripe tomato, halved
salt and pepper
8–12 basil leaves, to garnish

1 Preheat the grill on the hottest setting. Lay the peppers, courgettes and onion in a single layer on the grill rack. Brush with a little of the oil and rub with the garlic. Grill the vegetables on one side only, for about *5 minutes* or until lightly browned, but still firm. Set aside and keep warm.

2 Cut the bread diagonally into medium-thick slices and toast these on both sides. Rub the top of each slice with the garlic and tomato, then pile the grilled vegetables on top.

3 Trickle the remaining oil over the vegetables and season them well. Garnish with basil leaves and serve at once.

Preparation time: 10 minutes
Cooking time: 5 minutes
Serves 4

Aubergine, Tomato and Feta Rolls

2 medium aubergines
3 tablespoons olive oil
125 g (4 oz) feta cheese,
    coarsely diced

12 sun-dried tomatoes in oil,
    drained
15–20 basil leaves
salt and pepper

1 Trim the ends off the aubergines, then cut off a thin slice lengthways from both sides of each; discard these slices, which should be mainly skin. Cut each aubergine lengthways into 4 slices. Heat the grill on the hottest setting or heat a griddle pan on the hob.

2 Brush both sides of the aubergine slices with oil and grill them for about *3 minutes* on each side. Alternatively, cook them in the griddle pan, turning once, until browned and softened.

3 Lay the aubergine slices on a board and divide the cheese, tomatoes and basil leaves between them. Season well. Roll up the slices from the short ends and secure them with cocktail sticks. Arrange on serving plates and serve at once or cover and set aside in a cool place, but not the refrigerator.

Preparation time: 15 minutes
Cooking time: about 6 minutes
Serves 4

Smoked Salmon and Dill Cucumber Cones

2 small cucumbers, halved
  lengthways, deseeded and
  cut into thin strips
1 teaspoon English mustard
1 tablespoon white wine
  vinegar
½ teaspoon sugar

1 tablespoon finely chopped
  dill
2 wheat flour tortillas
4 tablespoons crème fraîche
125 g (4 oz) smoked salmon,
  cut into wide strips
salt and pepper

1 Put the cucumber in a shallow bowl. Mix the mustard, vinegar, sugar and dill. Season the mixture well, then pour it over the cucumbers. Leave to stand for *5 minutes*.

2 To assemble the cones, cut the tortillas in half and lay them on a board or work surface. Spread 1 tablespoon crème fraîche over each tortilla half.

3 Divide the smoked salmon strips between the tortillas and top with the cucumber mixture. Add a little seasoning, if liked, and roll up the tortillas to form cones around the filling. Secure each cone with a cocktail stick, if liked.

Preparation time: 15 minutes
Serves 4

Variation
There are endless variations on the combination of ingredients that can be wrapped up in this fashion. Chicken, mango and coriander makes a tasty and healthy lunch or quick snack.

Courgette Cakes with Minted Sauce and Salsa

500 g (1 lb) courgettes, finely grated
2 tablespoons mayonnaise
300 g (10 oz) fresh bread-crumbs
½ teaspoon ground cumin
½ teaspoon ground coriander
¼ teaspoon cayenne pepper
vegetable oil, for shallow-frying

MINTED SAUCE:
4 tablespoons finely chopped mint
finely grated rind and juice of 1 lime
150 ml (¼ pint) Greek yogurt

SALSA:
2 ripe plum tomatoes or tomatoes on the vine, deseeded and finely diced
½ cucumber, deseeded and finely diced
1 small red onion, finely chopped
1 tablespoon white wine vinegar
1 teaspoon sugar
salt and pepper

1 Put the grated courgettes in a colander and squeeze out as much liquid from them as possible. Then transfer them to a bowl. Add the mayonnaise, breadcrumbs, cumin, coriander and cayenne pepper. Season to taste and mix well. Set aside.

2 Mix the ingredients for the minted yogurt sauce in a serving bowl, adding seasoning to taste. Cover and chill until ready to serve.

3 Combine the ingredients for the salsa in a serving bowl and add seasoning to taste. Cover and chill until ready to serve.

4 Divide the courgette mixture into 12 equal portions. Heat the oil in a large nonstick frying pan. Place a portion of the mixture in the pan and flatten it to form a thick cake. Add as many portions as will fit in the pan, flattening each in the same way. Fry the cakes for *3–4 minutes* on each side or until lightly browned. Drain on kitchen paper and keep hot until all the mixture is cooked.

5 Serve the cakes hot with the cool sauce and salsa.

Preparation time: 20 minutes
Cooking time: 6–8 minutes
Serves 4

Vietnamese Salad Rolls with Dipping Sauce

12 small rice paper spring roll wrappers
1 carrot, cut into fine julienne
1 cucumber, halved length-ways, deseeded and cut into fine julienne
125 g (4 oz) enoki mushrooms or bean sprouts
2 spring onions, finely shredded
15 g (½ oz) mint leaves
15 g (½ oz) coriander leaves

DIPPING SAUCE:
2 tablespoons fish sauce
3 tablespoons lime juice
2 teaspoons caster sugar
1 small red chilli, deseeded (optional) and finely sliced

1 Soak the spring roll wrappers in hot water for *1–2 minutes* or until softened. Then drain well.

2 Lay the wrappers on a clean work surface or board and cover with a damp tea towel.

3 Divide the carrot, cucumber, enoki mushrooms or bean sprouts, spring onions, mint and coriander evenly between the wrappers. Fold and roll the wrappers around the salad filling to enclose it in neat packages. Place on a board and cover with a damp tea towel until ready to serve.

4 Mix all the ingredients for the dipping sauce and pour it into a small bowl. Arrange the salad rolls on a large platter or individual plates and serve with the dipping sauce.

Preparation time: 15 minutes
Serves 4

Grilled Herbed Oysters

12 oysters
1 garlic clove, crushed
1 tablespoon finely chopped
  flat leaf parsley
2 tablespoons fresh
  breadcrumbs
1 tablespoon finely chopped
  shallot
2 tablespoons lemon juice
25 g (1 oz) butter, softened
salt and pepper
lemon wedges, to serve

1 Use an oyster knife or short-bladed, heavy knife to open the oysters: cover your hand with an ovenglove for protection and hold an oyster with the deeper shell underneath. Insert the knife between the top and bottom shells at the point where they are hinged together and prise them apart, being careful not to lose any of the juices. Slide the knife around the edge and under the top shell, then discard the flatter top shell. Arrange the oyster with its liquor in the half-shell on a grill pan. Repeat with all the remaining oysters.

2 In a small mixing bowl, thoroughly mix the garlic, parsley, breadcrumbs, shallot, lemon juice and butter. Season well to taste. Divide the mixture between the oysters, placing a small dollop on top of each one.

3 Heat the grill on the hottest setting, then grill the oysters for *3–4 minutes* or until lightly browned. Serve at once, offering lemon wedges with the oysters.

Preparation time: 15 minutes
Cooking time: 3–4 minutes
Serves 4

Deep Fried Goats' Cheese with Rocket and Red Onion Marmalade

4 individual goats' cheeses,
  about 60 g (2½ oz) each
2 eggs, beaten
4 tablespoons fresh
  breadcrumbs
about 200 ml (7 fl oz)
  vegetable oil, for frying
125 g (4 oz) rocket leaves
2 tablespoons olive oil

RED ONION MARMALADE:
1 tablespoon olive oil
2 red onions, thinly sliced
125 ml (4 fl oz) red wine
3 tablespoons red wine
  vinegar
50 g (2 oz) caster sugar
salt and pepper

1 Dip the cheeses in beaten egg and then coat them evenly with the breadcrumbs. Chill the coated cheeses while you prepare the onion marmalade.

2 To make the marmalade, heat the olive oil in a small saucepan. Add the onions and cook gently for *2 minutes*. Stir in the wine, vinegar and sugar, then continue to cook gently for *5 minutes* or until the onions are translucent. Use a slotted spoon to remove the onions from the pan and set them aside on a plate; reserve the juices.

3 Heat the vegetable oil for frying in a nonstick frying pan to 180–190°C (350–375°F) or until a cube of bread browns in *30 seconds*. (There should be sufficient depth of oil to deep-fry the small cheeses, but take care not to overfill the frying pan. If necessary use a saucepan or deep-frying pan.) Fry the goats' cheeses for about *2 minutes* or until golden. Remove with a slotted spoon and drain well on kitchen paper.

4 Divide the rocket among 4 plates and drizzle the olive oil and reserved juice from the onions over the top. Season to taste. Place the fried goats' cheeses on the rocket and top with the onion marmalade. Serve at once.

Preparation time: 15 minutes
Cooking time: about 9 minutes
Serves 4

Salads and Vegetables

Substantial, tasty and healthy meals can quickly be prepared using the freshest vegetables and greens. The recipes in this chapter can be served as appetizers or accompaniments or on their own as a light supper.

Celery, Red Onion and New Potato Salad

This substantial salad is a kaleidoscope of vibrant and beautiful colours. It is the perfect salad to serve as a light dinner on a warm evening or as an accompaniment to grilled food.

500 g (1 lb) new potatoes,
   halved
1 small fennel bulb, halved,
   cored and finely sliced
2 celery sticks, thinly sliced
1 red onion, halved and thinly
   sliced

DRESSING:
150 ml (¼ pint) mayonnaise
2 teaspoons coarse-grain
   mustard
2 tablespoons finely chopped
   dill
salt and pepper
celery leaves or dill sprigs,
   to garnish (optional)

1 Add the potatoes to a large saucepan of boiling water and boil for *10–15 minutes* or until they are tender.

2 Meanwhile, mix the fennel, celery and onion in a large, shallow bowl and set aside.

3 To make the dressing, mix the mayonnaise, mustard and dill in a small bowl, adding seasoning to taste.

4 Drain the potatoes, rinse them under cool running water, then drain again. Add the potatoes to the salad. Add the dressing and toss the ingredients until they are well coated. Garnish with celery leaves or dill sprigs, if liked.

Preparation time: 10 minutes
Cooking time: 10–15 minutes
Serves 4

Grilled Aubergine and Courgette Salad with Honey-Mint Dressing

2 medium aubergines, thinly
   sliced
2 courgettes, thinly sliced
1 red pepper, cored, deseeded
   and cut into strips
about 3 tablespoons olive oil
125 g (4 oz) feta cheese

HONEY-MINT DRESSING:
50 g (2 oz) mint leaves,
   coarsely chopped
1 tablespoon clear honey
1 teaspoon prepared English
   mustard
2 tablespoons lime juice
salt and pepper
mint leaves, to garnish
toasted flat breads or crusty
   baguette, to serve

1 Brush the aubergine and courgette slices, and red pepper strips with olive oil. Heat the grill on the hottest setting and grill the vegetables for *2–3 minutes* on each side, until lightly cooked.

2 Arrange the grilled vegetables in a shallow dish. Crumble the feta cheese and sprinkle it over the vegetables.

3 Thoroughly mix the dressing ingredients in a small bowl, adding seasoning to taste. Pour the dressing over the salad.

4 Scatter the mint leaves over the salad as a garnish. Serve with toasted flat breads or crusty baguette.

Preparation time: 15 minutes
Cooking time: 4–6 minutes
Serves 4

Mediterranean Kebabs

These tasty kebabs can easily be adapted with a quick change of vegetables. Try using thick slices of fennel, cubes of aubergine and shiitake or button mushrooms.

2 courgettes
12 cherry tomatoes
1 red onion, cut into 8 wedges
1 red pepper, cored, deseeded and cut into 2.5 cm (1 inch) squares
2 tablespoons olive oil
1 tablespoon finely chopped flat leaf parsley

½ teaspoon chilli flakes
4 tablespoons lemon juice
1 garlic clove, crushed
salt and pepper
chopped thyme, to garnish
steamed rice or a crisp green salad and lemon wedges, to serve

1 Trim the courgettes, then use a vegetable peeler to cut them lengthways into very thin slices or ribbons. Place the courgettes in a shallow bowl and add the tomatoes, onion and pepper.

2 Mix the oil, parsley, chilli flakes, lemon juice, garlic and seasoning, then pour this mixture over the vegetables and set them aside to marinate for at least *5 minutes*.

3 Thread the vegetables on to 8 medium or 4 large metal skewers, making sure there is a variety of vegetables on each skewer and threading the strips of courgette between and around the other vegetables. Alternatively, you can roll up the courgette strips and thread the rolls on to the skewers. Reserve the juices from the marinade.

4 Heat the grill on the hottest setting. Brush the vegetables with the reserved seasoning mixture. Grill the kebabs, turning frequently, for about *6–8 minutes*, until the vegetables are cooked. Garnish with thyme and serve with rice or a salad and lemon wedges.

Preparation time: 20 minutes
Cooking time: 6–8 minutes
Serves 4

Panzanella

Panzanella is a traditional southern Italian dish and formed what was perhaps the original picnic lunch. The simple ingredients were taken into the fields by harvesters for their mid-day meal. It is also a good way to use up stale bread.

1 small loaf of crusty bread, preferably 1–2 days old
2 tablespoons capers or caperberries, rinsed and drained
8 plum tomatoes, coarsely chopped
2 red onions, halved and sliced
10 black olives, pitted
20 basil leaves
1 garlic clove, crushed
4 tablespoons olive oil
salt and pepper
Parmesan cheese shavings, to garnish (optional)

1 Cut the bread into large bite-sized chunks and put them in a bowl. Pour over a little cold water to moisten the bread, then drain the bread in a colander, squeezing the chunks dry.

2 Put the bread in a large salad bowl and mix in the capers or caperberries, tomatoes, onions, olives and basil.

3 In a small bowl, mix the garlic and olive oil together and season well. Pour this flavoured oil over the salad and toss well. Garnish with Parmesan shavings, if liked.

Preparation time: 10 minutes
Serves 4

Spiced Vegetable Couscous

2 tablespoons olive oil
1 onion, finely chopped
1 teaspoon ground cumin
½ teaspoon cayenne pepper
½ teaspoon ground cinnamon
2 garlic cloves, crushed
2 small carrots, cut into bite-sized chunks
1 courgette, thickly sliced
200 g (7 oz) can chickpeas, drained
1 red pepper, deseeded and coarsely diced
50 g (2 oz) ready-to-eat dried apricots
500 ml (17 fl oz) boiling vegetable stock
400 ml (14 fl oz) water
250 g (8 oz) couscous
4 tablespoons coarsely chopped coriander leaves
salt and pepper

1 Heat the oil in a large frying pan. Add the onion and cook gently for *3–4 minutes*, until it is soft but not browned.

2 Stir in the cumin, cayenne, cinnamon and garlic. Cook, stirring, for a further *1 minute*. Add the carrots, courgette, chickpeas, red pepper and apricots and cook, stirring, for *2–3 minutes*.

3 Pour in the boiling stock and bring back to the boil. Reduce the heat, cover the pan and simmer the vegetables gently for *8–10 minutes*.

4 Meanwhile, bring the water to the boil in a saucepan. Add the couscous, stir and remove from the heat. Cover and set aside until the vegetables are ready.

5 Check the vegetables for seasoning and stir in the chopped coriander. Fluff up the couscous with a fork and add seasoning to taste. Divide the couscous among 4 serving plates and ladle the vegetables with their broth over the top. Serve at once.

Preparation time: 15 minutes
Cooking time: 14–18 minutes
Serves 4

Garlic and Herb Mushrooms

3 tablespoons olive oil
12 open-cup or flat-cap
   mushrooms
2 garlic cloves, thinly sliced
2 tablespoons lemon juice

3 tablespoons finely chopped
   flat leaf parsley
salt and pepper
shavings of pecorino or
   Parmesan cheese, to serve

1 Heat the oil in a large nonstick frying pan. Fry the mushrooms over a high heat, turning once, until they start to colour.

2 Add the garlic and fry for *1–2 minutes*. Sprinkle in the lemon juice and parsley, stir to mix well, then add seasoning to taste.

3 Arrange the mushrooms on individual serving plates and pour the pan juices over them. Top with shavings of pecorino or Parmesan and serve at once.

Preparation time: 10 minutes
Cooking time: 5 minutes
Serves 4

Chickpea and Tomato Salad with Lemon Dressing

2 x 400 g (13 oz) cans chickpeas, drained and rinsed
2 plum tomatoes, coarsely
   chopped
4 spring onions, finely sliced
1 red chilli, deseeded and
   finely sliced
4 tablespoons coarsely
   chopped coriander leaves
grilled pitta bread, cut into
   thin fingers, to serve

LEMON DRESSING:
2 tablespoons lemon juice
1 garlic clove, crushed
2 tablespoons olive oil
salt and pepper

1 Combine all the salad ingredients in a shallow bowl.

2 To make the dressing, mix the lemon juice, garlic and olive oil with a generous sprinkling of seasoning in a screw-top jar. Shake until thoroughly combined, then pour the dressing over the salad and toss well to coat all the ingredients.

3 Cover the salad and leave it to stand at room temperature for about *5–10 minutes* before serving to allow the flavours to develop and blend. Serve with the grilled pitta bread.

Preparation time: 10 minutes, plus standing
Serves 4

Variation
Canned chickpeas are a useful ingredient to keep stocked in the cupboard. They are already cooked, so only require rinsing before eating. They can also be eaten hot; just add to a saucepan of cold water and bring to the boil. Drain and serve in salads or with mixed vegetables.

Goats' Cheese, Pinenut and Cherry Tomato Tarts

4 filo pastry sheets, each
    about 25 cm (10 inches)
    square
1 tablespoon olive oil
20 cherry tomatoes, halved
200 g (7 oz) goat's cheese, cut
    into 1 cm (½ inch) cubes
20 g (¾ oz) pine nuts
2 teaspoons fresh thyme
    leaves
salt and pepper
leafy greens, such as leaf beet
    or spinach, to serve

1 Lightly grease 4 individual tartlet tins, each about 10 cm (4 inches) in diameter. Brush a sheet of filo pastry with a little olive oil. Cut it in half, then across into 4 equal-sized squares and use these to line one of the tins. Repeat with the remaining pastry. Brush any remaining oil over the pastry in the tins.

2 Place 5 tomato halves in the bottom of each tartlet. Top with the cheese, then add the remaining tomato halves and pine nuts. Sprinkle with the thyme leaves and season well.

3 Bake the tartlets in a preheated oven, 200°C (400°F), Gas Mark 6, for *10–12 minutes* or until the pastry is crisp and golden. Serve hot with a leafy green salad.

Preparation time: 15 minutes
Cooking time: 10–12 minutes
Serves 4

Cook's Tip
Use firm goat's cheese as the very soft variety tends to liquify when cooked.

Courgette and Mint Frittata

2 tablespoons olive oil
1 red onion, thinly sliced
500 g (1 lb) courgettes, thinly
    sliced
1 red chilli, deseeded and
    thinly sliced
5 eggs, beaten
1 tablespoon double cream
4 tablespoons chopped mint
50 g (2 oz) Parmesan cheese,
    grated
salt and pepper
grilled foccacia bread, or
    warmed crusty bread,
    to serve

1 Heat the oil in a 20 cm (8 inch) frying pan. Add the onion and cook over a moderate heat for about *3–4 minutes*, stirring, until softened slightly. Add the courgettes and the chilli, then increase the heat to high and cook for *4–5 minutes*.

2 Meanwhile, beat the eggs with the cream, adding seasoning to taste and the mint. Pour the eggs over the mixture. Reduce the heat to medium and cook for about *5 minutes* or until just set on top and golden underneath. Use a spatula or fish slice to lift the edge of the mixture to check that it is browned underneath.

3 Sprinkle the Parmesan over the frittata and place it under a hot grill for *3–4 minutes* or until the frittata is golden and set.

4 Serve the frittata cut into wedges, on grilled foccacia bread, or with warmed crusty bread and a tomato salad, if liked.

Preparation time: 10 minutes
Cooking time: 15–18 minutes
Serves 4

Dolcelatte and Leek Galette

8 thin leeks
300 g (10 oz) puff pastry
50 ml (2 fl oz) crème fraîche
1 teaspoon cayenne pepper
1 tablespoon coarse-grain
   mustard

50 g (2 oz) dolcelatte cheese,
   crumbled
1 egg, beaten
salt and pepper
chopped parsley, to garnish
   (optional)

1 Trim the leeks to 20 cm (8 inches) in length and put them in a large frying pan. Pour in just enough boiling water to cover the leeks and bring back to the boil. Reduce the heat, cover the pan and simmer for *5–7 minutes*. Drain the leeks and set them aside.

2 Meanwhile, line a baking sheet with nonstick baking paper. Roll out the pastry into a square measuring about 25 cm (10 inches) on each side. Using a sharp knife, score the pastry 3.5 cm (1½ inches) from the edge all around the square to make a border. Take care not to cut right through the pastry. Transfer the pastry to the prepared baking sheet.

3 Pat the leeks dry with kitchen paper to remove any excess moisture and arrange them on the pastry, inside the border.

4 Mix the crème fraîche, cayenne, mustard and cheese until thoroughly combined. Gently spread this mixture over the leeks. Season well and cook in a preheated oven, 220°C (425°F), Gas Mark 7, for *15 minutes* or until the pastry has risen and the border is browned.

5 Cut the galette into quarters and sprinkle each portion with chopped parsley, if using. Serve at once.

Preparation time: 15 minutes
Cooking time: 20–22 minutes
Serves 4

Grilled Chicory with Salsa Verde

4 heads of treviso or chicory,
   each about 150 g (5 oz),
   trimmed and halved
   lengthways
2 tablespoons olive oil
125 g (4 oz) Parmesan cheese,
   coarsely grated
chopped parsley, to garnish
toasted ciabatta bread,
   to serve

SALSA VERDE:
200 g (7 oz) flat leaf parsley
50 g (2 oz) pine nuts, toasted
2 pickled gherkins
8 green olives, pitted
1 garlic clove, chopped
1 tablespoon lemon juice
150 ml (¼ pint) olive oil
salt and pepper

1 First make the salsa verde: coarsely purée all the ingredients, except the oil, in a food processor or blender. With the motor still running, gradually trickle in the oil to make a creamy paste. Transfer to a serving dish, cover and set aside. (The salsa will keep for up to 1 week in the refrigerator.)

2 Heat the grill on the hottest setting. Place the treviso or chicory halves on the grill rack, cut sides down, brush with some of the oil and grill for *5 minutes*. Turn the vegetables, brush with the remaining oil and sprinkle the Parmesan over the top. Grill for a further *4 minutes* or until the cheese has melted and the edges begin to char.

3 Transfer the treviso or chicory to plates and garnish with chopped parsley. Add a little salsa verde to each plate and serve immediately, offering the remaining salsa verde separately. Toasted ciabatta bread is a good accompaniment.

Preparation time: 15 minutes
Cooking time: 9 minutes
Serves 4

Pasta and Grains

The infinite number of fantastic recipes that can be prepared in under 30 minutes with pasta, rice and other grains makes them essential ingredients for all kitchens. You need never order a take-away again!

Pasta with Chilli, Coriander and Cashew Nut Pesto

You can use basically any type of dried or fresh pasta with this rich and creamy sauce. Fresh pasta is ideal to use when time is very short as it cooks in minutes.

400 g (13 oz) dried fusilli
  lunghi, linguine or other
  long thin pasta
50 g (2 oz) coriander leaves,
  coarsely chopped
2 garlic cloves, coarsely
  chopped
50 g (2 oz) roasted cashew
  nuts
1 green chilli, deseeded and
  coarsely chopped

125 ml (4 fl oz) olive oil
50 g (2 oz) Parmesan cheese,
  grated
salt and pepper

TO SERVE:
crusty bread
a crisp tomato or green salad

1 Cook the pasta in a large saucepan of boiling salted water for *8–10 minutes* or according to the packet instructions, until *al dente*, tender, but with bite.

2 Meanwhile, process the coriander leaves, garlic, cashew nuts, chilli and olive oil in a blender or food processor until fairly smooth and creamy. Add the cheese and process for a few seconds. Transfer the pesto to a bowl, season well and set aside.

3 Drain the pasta and return it to the pan. Add the pesto and mix well. Serve at once, with crusty bread and a crisp salad.

Preparation time: 10 minutes
Cooking time: 8–10 minutes
Serves 4

Summer Vegetable Fettuccine

250 g (8 oz) asparagus,
  trimmed and cut into
  5 cm (2 inch) lengths
125 g (4 oz) sugarsnap peas
400 g (13 oz) dried fettuccine
  or pappardelle
200 g (7 oz) baby courgettes
150 g (5 oz) button mushrooms
1 tablespoon olive oil

1 small onion, finely chopped
1 garlic clove, finely chopped
4 tablespoons lemon juice
2 teaspoons chopped tarragon
2 teaspoons chopped parsley
100 g (3½ oz) smoked
  mozzarella cheese, diced
salt and pepper
garlic bread, to serve

1 Bring a saucepan of water to the boil. Add the asparagus and sugarsnap peas and boil for *3–4 minutes*, then drain and refresh with cold water. Drain well and set aside.

2 Cook the fettuccine or pappardelle in a large saucepan of boiling salted water for *8–10 minutes* or according to the packet instructions, until *al dente*, tender, but with bite.

3 Meanwhile, halve the courgettes lengthways and cut the mushrooms in half. Heat the oil in a large frying pan. Add the onion and garlic, and cook gently for about *2–3 minutes*. Add the courgettes and mushrooms and fry, stirring, for *3–4 minutes*. Stir in the asparagus and sugarsnap peas and cook for *1–2 minutes* before adding the lemon juice, tarragon and parsley.

4 Drain the pasta and return it to the pan. Add the vegetable mixture and mozzarella and season to taste. Toss lightly to mix, then serve at once with hot garlic bread.

Preparation time: 10 minutes
Cooking time: 17–23 minutes
Serves 4

Paella

200 g (7 oz) mussels in shells
2 tablespoons olive oil
1 onion, finely chopped
100 g (3½ oz) pancetta, cut into
    small cubes
2 garlic cloves, finely chopped
1 red pepper, cored, deseeded
    and coarsely chopped
200 g (7 oz) long-grain rice

900 ml (1½ pints) chicken
    stock
1 teaspoon turmeric
1 teaspoon paprika, preferably
    sweet smoked paprika
200 g (7 oz) raw tiger prawns,
    peeled, with tails intact
125 g (4 oz) frozen peas
salt and pepper
chopped parsley, to garnish

1 First prepare the mussels. Scrub the mussels in cold water, scrape off any barnacles and pull away any of the dark hairy beards that protrude from the shells. Discard any broken shells or open mussels that do not close when tapped sharply. Put the mussels in a heavy-based saucepan with 75 ml (3 fl oz) of boiling water and shake over a brisk heat until all the shells have opened. Drain and discard any shells that do not open. Set aside.

2 Heat the oil in a large nonstick frying pan. Add the onion and pancetta, and cook gently for *5 minutes*.

3 Add the garlic, red pepper and rice, and fry for *1–2 minutes*. Pour in the stock, then stir in the turmeric and paprika. Bring to the boil, cover the pan and reduce the heat. Simmer gently for about *10–12 minutes*.

4 Stir in the prawns, mussels and peas. Cover and cook for a further *5 minutes*. Season well, garnish with chopped parsley and serve at once.

Preparation time: 15 minutes
Cooking time: 25–27 minutes
Serves 4

Cook's Tip
This recipe uses fresh mussels which do take a bit of time to prepare. You can substitute the fresh mussels with good-quality bottled mussels – a versatile and convenient ingredient to keep in the cupboard.

Quick Pasta Carbonara

400 g (13 oz) dried spaghetti
   or other long thin pasta
2 tablespoons olive oil
1 onion, finely chopped
200 g (7 oz) pancetta, cut
   into cubes
2 garlic cloves, finely chopped
3 eggs

4 tablespoons grated
   Parmesan cheese
3 tablespoons chopped flat
   leaf parsley
3 tablespoons single cream
salt and pepper
green salad, to serve
   (optional)

1 Cook the pasta in a large saucepan of boiling salted water for *8–10 minutes* or according to the packet instructions, until *al dente*, tender but with bite.

2 Meanwhile, heat the oil in a large nonstick frying pan. Add the onion and fry until it is soft. Then add the pancetta and garlic, and cook gently for *4–5 minutes*.

3 Beat the eggs with the Parmesan, parsley and cream. Season to taste and set aside.

4 Drain the pasta and add it to the onion and pancetta. Stir over a gentle heat until combined, then pour in the egg mixture. Stir and remove the pan from the heat. Continue mixing well for a few seconds, until the eggs are lightly cooked and creamy. Serve immediately. A green salad goes well with creamy carbonara.

Preparation time: 10 minutes
Cooking time: 8–10 minutes
Serves 4

Jewelled Tabbouleh

3 tablespoons olive oil
1 large onion, coarsely
   chopped
300 g (10 oz) bulgar wheat
750 ml (1¼ pints) vegetable
   stock
50 g (2 oz) pine nuts, toasted
4 dried apricots, coarsely
   chopped

seeds from 1 small
   pomegranate
4 tablespoons coarsely
   chopped mint
1 tablespoon lemon juice
salt and pepper
mint leaves, to garnish

1 Heat 1 tablespoon of the oil in a saucepan, add the onion and cook briskly, stirring often, until it is soft. Add the bulgar wheat and the stock and bring to the boil. Cover the pan, reduce the heat and simmer gently for *15 minutes*, stirring occasionally, or until the stock is absorbed and the wheat is tender.

2 Turn the bulgar wheat into a large serving bowl. Mix in the pine nuts, apricots, pomegranate seeds and chopped mint.

3 In a small bowl, mix the remaining oil with the lemon juice, then pour this dressing over the wheat mixture. Season to taste and toss until well mixed. Garnish with mint leaves before serving.

Preparation time: 15 minutes
Cooking time: about 20 minutes
Serves 4

Variation
This dish is equally delicious using couscous or good-quality cooked, cooled rice instead of the bulgar wheat.

Lemon and Chilli Prawn Linguine

375 g (12 oz) dried linguine
    or spaghetti
1 tablespoon olive oil
15 g (½ oz) butter
1 garlic clove, finely chopped
2 spring onions, thinly sliced
2 red chillies, deseeded and
    thinly sliced

450 g (14½ oz) raw tiger
    prawns, peeled, with tails
    left intact
2 tablespoons lemon juice
2 tablespoons finely chopped
    coriander leaves
salt and pepper

1 Cook the pasta in a large saucepan of boiling salted water for *8–10 minutes* or according to the packet instructions, until *al dente*, tender, but with bite.

2 When the pasta is about half cooked, heat the oil and butter in a large nonstick frying pan. Add the garlic, spring onions and chillies, and stir-fry for *2–3 minutes*.

3 Add the prawns and cook briskly for *3–4 minutes* or until they turn pink and are just cooked through. Pour in the lemon juice and stir in the coriander until well mixed, then remove from the heat and set aside.

4 Drain the pasta and toss it with the prawn mixture, either in the frying pan (if it is large enough) or in a large serving bowl. Season well and serve hot.

Preparation time: 15 minutes
Cooking time: about 10 minutes
Serves 4

Herbed Couscous with Tomato, Cucumber and Mixed Nuts

250 g (8 oz) couscous
400 ml (14 fl oz) boiling
    vegetable stock
4 plum tomatoes, chopped
1 cucumber, deseeded and
    coarsely chopped
3 spring onions, thinly sliced
4 tablespoons coarsely
    chopped mint

4 tablespoons coarsely
    chopped coriander leaves
125 g (4 oz) nuts (mix of
    walnuts and cashew nuts)
125 g (4 oz) feta cheese, diced
3 tablespoons olive oil
4 tablespoons lemon juice
salt and pepper
Greek yogurt, to serve

1 Put the couscous in a deep bowl and pour in the boiling stock. Cover and leave to stand for *10 minutes*, by which time the couscous will have absorbed all the stock.

2 Meanwhile, mix the tomatoes, cucumber, spring onions, mint, chopped coriander, nuts, feta, oil and lemon juice in a large bowl.

3 Fluff up the couscous with a fork. Add the vegetable mixture to the couscous. Season well to taste and fork the vegetables through the couscous until well mixed. Serve at once, while hot, adding a dollop of yogurt to each portion.

Preparation time: 20 minutes, plus standing
Serves 4

Polenta with Wild Mushrooms

175 g (6 oz) instant polenta
15 g (½ oz) butter
600 ml (1 pint) water
3 tablespoons olive oil
1 onion, chopped
475 g (15 oz) mixed wild
   mushrooms, thickly sliced
1 garlic clove, crushed
1 tablespoon sun-dried
   tomato purée

2 teaspoons thyme leaves
125 ml (4 fl oz) red wine
50 ml (2 fl oz) brandy
1 tablespoon coarsely
   chopped flat leaf parsley
salt and pepper

GARNISH (OPTIONAL):
parsley sprigs
thyme sprigs

1 Put the polenta and butter in a saucepan. Pour in the water, season to taste and bring to the boil, stirring continuously. Reduce the heat and cook gently for *8 minutes*, occasionally stirring, to remove any lumps that may form.

2 Meanwhile, heat the oil in a large saucepan. Add the onion and fry for *3–4 minutes*, then add the mushrooms and garlic. Cook briskly for *5–6 minutes*.

3 Stir the sun-dried tomato purée, thyme, wine and brandy into the mushroom mixture. Bring to the boil and cook briskly for about *10 minutes*.

4 Stir the parsley into the mushrooms and season the mixture well. To serve, arrange spoonfuls of the polenta on individual plates and spoon the mushroom sauce over. Garnish with parsley and thyme, if using, and serve at once.

Preparation time: 5 minutes
Cooking time: 15–16 minutes
Serves 4

Beetroot Risotto

1 tablespoon olive oil
15 g (½ oz) butter
1 teaspoon crushed or
   coarsely ground coriander
   seeds
4 spring onions, thinly sliced
400 g (13 oz) freshly cooked
   beetroot, cut into 1 cm
   (½ inch) dice
500 g (1 lb) arborio rice

1.5 litres (2½ pints) hot
   vegetable stock
200 g (7 oz) cream cheese
4 tablespoons finely chopped
   dill
salt and pepper

GARNISH (OPTIONAL):
dill sprigs
a little crème fraîche

1 Heat the oil and butter in a large, heavy-based saucepan about 25 cm (10 inches). Add the crushed coriander seeds and spring onions, and stir-fry briskly for *1 minute*.

2 Add the beetroot and the rice. Cook, stirring, for *2–3 minutes* to coat all the grains with oil and butter. Gradually pour in the hot stock, a ladleful at a time, cooking and stirring often until each ladleful is absorbed before adding the next. This should take about *20 minutes*, by which time the rice should be *al dente*, tender, but still firm to the bite.

3 Stir in the cream cheese and dill, and season to taste. Serve immediately, garnished with dill sprigs and a little crème fraîche, if using.

Preparation time: 5–10 minutes
Cooking time: about 23–24 minutes
Serves 4

Cook's Tip
Depending on the quality and variety of rice used, you may need to adjust the quantity of stock. Keep some extra hot stock or water at hand in case you need to add more to the pan before the rice is fully cooked.

Meat and Poultry

A selection of quick-cooking meat cuts are used in this chapter as well as quick cooking methods to create scrumptious meals that look and taste as though they took hours, rather than minutes, to prepare.

Spicy Pork Rolls with Minted Yogurt

4 pork escalopes, about
    125–150 g (4–5 oz) each
1 small onion, coarsely chopped
1 red chilli, deseeded and
    coarsely chopped
4 tablespoons coarsely
    chopped coriander leaves
grated rind and juice of 1 lime
1 tablespoon fish sauce
2 garlic cloves, crushed
1 teaspoon grated fresh ginger

1 teaspoon ground cumin
½ teaspoon ground coriander
50 ml (2 fl oz) coconut milk
salt and pepper
mint leaves, to garnish
    (optional)

MINTED YOGURT:
4 tablespoons coarsely
    chopped mint leaves
200 ml (7 fl oz) Greek yogurt

1 Lay a pork escalope between 2 sheets of clingfilm and beat it out with a mallet to a thickness of 5 mm (¼ inch). Repeat with the remaining escalopes.

2 Process the remaining ingredients to a coarse paste in a blender or food processor. Spread a quarter of the paste over a thin pork escalope and roll up to enclose the filling. Secure the roll with a wooden cocktail stick. Repeat with the remaining paste and pork.

3 Place the rolls on a baking sheet and cook in a preheated oven, 200°C (400°F), Gas Mark 6, for about *10–12 minutes* or until cooked through.

4 Meanwhile, make the minted yogurt by mixing the mint into the yogurt and adding seasoning to taste. Serve the rolls hot, with a dollop of the minted yogurt on the side and garnished with mint leaves, if liked.

Preparation time: 15 minutes
Cooking time: 10–12 minutes
Serves 4

Variation
The spicy rolls are equally very tasty using chicken breast fillets instead of the pork. Use the same quantity.

Pork Stroganoff

3 tablespoons olive oil
6 spring onions, thinly sliced
300 g (10 oz) mushrooms,
    thickly sliced
500 g (1 lb) pork fillet, cut into
    thin strips
1 tablespoon green
    peppercorns, crushed
2 tablespoons coarse-grain
    mustard

300 ml (½ pint) soured cream
100 g (3½ oz) pickled gherkins,
    coarsely chopped
4 tablespoons finely snipped
    chives
salt and pepper
buttered noodles or boiled
    rice, to serve

1 Heat 1 tablespoon of the oil in a large nonstick frying pan. Add the spring onions and fry, stirring, for *2–3 minutes* or until soft and then add the mushrooms. Cook briskly for *5 minutes*. Transfer this mixture to a bowl, cover and set aside.

2 Wipe out the pan with kitchen paper, then add and heat the remaining oil. Add the pork and fry for *3–4 minutes*, stirring to brown the strips evenly.

3 Return the mushroom mixture with its juices to the pan and add the peppercorns. Mix the mustard, soured cream and gherkins and stir this into the pork, then heat gently, without boiling. Stir in the chives and seasoning to taste. Serve hot with buttered noodles or boiled rice.

Preparation time: 10 minutes
Cooking time: 10–12 minutes
Serves 4

Steaks in a Pink and Green Peppercorn Sauce with Rosemary Mash

1 tablespoon vegetable oil
15 g (½ oz) butter
4 sirloin steaks, about 200 g (7 oz) each
250 ml (8 fl oz) double cream
1 tablespoon coarse-grain mustard
1 tablespoon pink peppercorns
1 tablespoon green peppercorns
1 tablespoon chopped flat leaf parsley

ROSEMARY MASH:
6 large Desirée or King Edward potatoes, peeled and cut into small cubes
1 garlic clove, crushed
2 tablespoons finely chopped rosemary leaves
4 tablespoons crème fraîche
salt and pepper

1 First make the rosemary mash. Cook the potatoes in a large saucepan of boiling, lightly salted water for *8–10 minutes*, until tender.

2 Drain the potatoes through a colander and return them to the pan. Mash until smooth, then stir in the garlic, rosemary and crème fraîche. Season well, set aside and keep hot, if necessary.

3 While the potatoes are cooking, heat a large nonstick frying pan until very hot. Add the oil and butter. When the butter has melted, add the steaks. Cook for *3 minutes*, then turn and cook for *2 minutes* if you like your steak rare, *3 minutes* for a medium-cooked result or *4 minutes* if you prefer steak well done.

4 Transfer the steaks to warmed serving plates and keep hot. Stir the cream into the cooking juices remaining in the pan and bring to a boil. Add the mustard and the pink and green pepper-corns and stir until well mixed. Stir in the parsley and add seasoning to taste.

5 Pour the hot sauce over the steaks. Add spoonfuls of the rosemary mash on the side and serve at once.

Preparation time: 10 minutes
Cooking time: 8–10 minutes
Serves 4

Lamb Cutlets with Garlic Crushed Potatoes

8 lamb cutlets, trimmed
1 tablespoon olive oil
2 garlic cloves, finely chopped
2 tablespoons finely chopped rosemary
2 teaspoons freshly ground black pepper
2 teaspoons sea salt

GARLIC CRUSHED POTATOES:
6 large Desirée potatoes, coarsely chopped
2 teaspoons crushed garlic
4 tablespoons crème fraîche
salt and pepper
fresh rosemary, to garnish

1 Place the lamb cutlets in a large shallow dish. Mix the olive oil, garlic, rosemary, pepper and sea salt, then pour this mixture over the cutlets. Make sure that all the meat is well coated. Cover and set aside.

2 Cook the potatoes in a large saucepan of boiling salted water for *8–10 minutes* or until just tender. Drain the potatoes in a colander and return them to the pan.

3 Mix the crushed garlic into the crème fraîche and season well, then add to the potatoes. Lightly crush the potatoes with a spoon. Cover and keep warm.

4 To cook the cutlets, heat a grill on the hottest setting. Lay the cutlets on the grill rack and cook for *3–4 minutes* on each side or until cooked to your liking. Serve at once, with the garlic crushed potatoes and rosemary to garnish.

Preparation time: 15 minutes
Cooking time: 14–18 minutes
Serves 4

Veal Escalopes with Lemon and Thyme Cream

2 tablespoons plain flour
4 veal escalopes, about
    125 g (4 oz) each
2 tablespoons olive oil
60 g (2½ oz) butter
grated rind and juice of
    1 lemon
2 tablespoons fresh thyme
    leaves
6 tablespoons double cream
salt and pepper

TO SERVE:
sliced red onion and mixed
    leaf salad or steamed green
    vegetables

1 Put the flour into a shallow bowl or on a plate and season well. Coat the escalopes on both sides with the seasoned flour.

2 Heat the oil and butter in a large nonstick frying pan and fry the veal escalopes for about *2 minutes* on each side. Use a slotted spoon to transfer the veal to a plate, cover and keep warm.

3 Add the lemon rind and juice to the juices in the pan. Stir in the thyme and cook gently for *2 minutes*. Pour in the cream and cook over a gentle heat for *2–3 minutes*.

4 Return the veal escalopes to the pan and cook them in the sauce for *1 minute* on each side. Serve hot with a red onion and mixed leaf salad or steamed green vegetables.

Preparation time: 5 minutes
Cooking time: 10–11 minutes
Serves 4

Peppered Chicken Skewers with Rosemary

4 boneless, skinless chicken
    breasts
2 tablespoons finely chopped
    rosemary
2 garlic cloves, finely chopped
3 tablespoons lemon juice
2 teaspoons prepared English
    mustard
1 tablespoon clear honey
2 teaspoons freshly ground
    black pepper
1 tablespoon olive oil
salt
mixed leaf salad, to serve

1 Lay a chicken breast between 2 sheets of clingfilm, then flatten it slightly with a mallet or rolling pin. Cut the chicken into thick strips. Repeat with the remaining chicken breasts.

2 Put the chicken strips in a large shallow bowl. Add all the remaining ingredients and mix well. Cover and set aside to marinate for *5–10 minutes*.

3 Heat the grill on the hottest setting. Thread the chicken strips on to 8 metal skewers and grill for *4–5 minutes* on each side or until the chicken is cooked through. Serve at once with a salad, such as baby spinach leaves or lamb's lettuce with red onion.

Preparation time: 10 minutes plus marinating
Cooking time: 8–10 minutes
Serves 4

Variation
To create Greek Chicken Kebabs, substitute the rosemary with chopped thyme leaves and omit the English mustard. Serve with a feta cheese and tomato salad.

Honey-Soy Duck Breasts with Plum and Mango Salsa

4 duck breasts
2 tablespoons dark soy sauce
1 tablespoon clear honey
**1 teaspoon grated fresh root
   ginger**
1 teaspoon chilli powder

PLUM AND MANGO SALSA:
**1 large ripe mango, peeled,
   stoned and finely diced**
**6–8 plums, stoned and finely
   diced**
grated rind and juice of 1 lime
**1 small red onion, finely
   chopped**
1 tablespoon olive oil
**1 tablespoon coarsely
   chopped mint leaves**
**1 tablespoon coarsely
   chopped coriander**
salt and pepper

1 Use a sharp knife to score the skin on the duck breasts lightly, cutting down into the fat but not through to the meat.

2 Heat a frying pan until very hot, then lay the duck breasts in it, skin sides down, and cook for *3 minutes*, until sealed and browned. Turn the breasts over and cook for *2 minutes*. Use a slotted spoon to transfer the duck breasts to a baking sheet, arranging them skin sides up.

3 Mix the soy sauce, honey, ginger and chilli powder in a small bowl. Spoon this mixture over the duck and cook in a preheated oven, 200°C (400°F), Gas Mark 6, for *6–9 minutes*, until cooked to your liking. The duck may be served pink in the middle or more well cooked.

4 Meanwhile, combine all the ingredients for the salsa in a bowl and season well.

5 Thinly slice the cooked duck and fan out the slices slightly on individual plates. Spoon some of the salsa over the duck and serve at once, offering the remaining salsa separately.

Preparation time: 15 minutes
Cooking time: 11–14 minutes
Serves 4

Chicken and Spinach Masala

2 tablespoons vegetable oil
1 onion, thinly sliced
2 garlic cloves, crushed
1 green chilli, deseeded and thinly sliced
1 teaspoon finely grated fresh root ginger
1 teaspoon ground coriander
1 teaspoon ground cumin
200 g (7 oz) can tomatoes
750 g (1¾ lb) chicken thighs, skinned, boned and cut into bite-sized chunks

200 ml (7 fl oz) crème fraîche
300 g (10 oz) spinach, coarsely chopped
2 tablespoons chopped coriander leaves
salt and pepper

TO SERVE:

warmed naan bread or boiled basmati rice
chutneys or fresh mixed vegetable salad

1 Heat the oil in a large heavy-based saucepan. Add the onion, garlic, chilli and ginger. Stir-fry for *2–3 minutes* and then add the ground coriander and cumin. Stir and cook for another *1 minute*.

2 Pour in the tomatoes with their juice and cook gently for *3 minutes*. Increase the heat and add the chicken. Cook, stirring, until the outside of the chicken is sealed. Then stir in the crème fraîche and spinach.

3 Cover the pan and cook the chicken mixture gently for *6–8 minutes*, stirring occasionally. Stir in the coriander with seasoning to taste. Serve hot with naan bread or basmati rice, chutneys or a mixed vegetable salad, such as chopped red onion and cucumber.

Preparation time: 15 minutes
Cooking time: 13–16 minutes
Serves 4

Chicken Biryani

250 g (8 oz) chicken thighs, skinned and boned
1 teaspoon turmeric
1 teaspoon ground cumin
1 teaspoon ground coriander
1 teaspoon chilli powder
6 tablespoons Greek yogurt
1 tablespoon vegetable oil
1 onion, thinly sliced
2 garlic cloves, finely chopped
1 teaspoon grated fresh root ginger
5 cm (2 inch) piece of cinnamon stick

3 cloves
3 green cardamom pods
250 g (8 oz) basmati rice
600 ml (1 pint) chicken stock
400 g (13 oz) potatoes, peeled and cut into 2.5 cm (1 inch) chunks
salt and pepper

TO SERVE:

tomato and cucumber salad
poppadums
Indian pickles or chutneys

1 Cut the chicken into bite-sized chunks and place them in a bowl. Add the turmeric, cumin, coriander, chilli and yogurt, and mix well.

2 Heat the oil in a heavy-based saucepan. Add the onion, garlic, ginger, cinnamon, cloves and cardamoms, and fry for *3–4 minutes*.

3 Add the chicken mixture and cook for *2–3 minutes*, stirring often. Then stir in the rice and pour in the stock. Season well and bring to the boil. Add the potatoes, cover the pan tightly and reduce the heat. Simmer gently for *10–12 minutes*.

4 Remove the pan from the heat and leave it to stand, without removing the lid, for *5 minutes*. Fluff up the rice with a fork and serve with a tomato and cucumber salad, poppadums and Indian pickles or chutneys.

Preparation time: 15 minutes
Cooking time: 15–19 minutes, plus standing
Serves 4

Chicken on Lemon Grass Skewers

The flavour of the lemon grass is released as they cook, infusing an incredible perfume and subtle spice into the chicken.

300 g (10 oz) minced chicken
1 garlic clove, crushed
1 teaspoon grated fresh root ginger
1 tablespoon fish sauce
2 teaspoons ground cumin
2 teaspoons ground coriander
1 tablespoon finely chopped fresh coriander leaves
1 red chilli, deseeded and finely chopped

1 teaspoon sugar
grated rind and juice of 1 lime
1 tablespoon desiccated coconut
salt and pepper
8 lemon grass stalks

TO SERVE:
boiled rice
a mixed salad

1 Put all the ingredients except the lemon grass in a bowl. Season well, then use your hands to pound and press the mixture together until thoroughly blended. Cover and chill for *10 minutes*.

2 When you are ready to cook the skewers, divide the chicken mixture into 8 equal-sized portions. Mould a portion of mixture on to the end of a lemon grass stalk, forming a sausage shape. Repeat with the remaining portions of mixture and lemon grass.

3 Heat the grill on the hottest setting and cook the skewers for *5–6 minutes* on each side or until the chicken mixture is cooked through. Serve hot, with boiled rice and a mixed salad.

Preparation time: 15 minutes
Cooking time: 10–12 minutes
Serves 4

Pesto Turkey Kebabs

4 turkey breast steaks, about 500 g (1 lb) in total
2 tablespoons pesto
8 slices of Parma ham
125 g (4 oz) sun-dried tomatoes, finely chopped

125 g (4 oz) mozzarella cheese, finely diced
1 tablespoon olive oil
salt and pepper
chopped parsley, to garnish
lemon wedges, to serve

1 Place a turkey steak between 2 sheets of clingfilm and pound it lightly with a mallet until it is about 1 cm (½ inch) thick. Repeat with the remaining steaks.

2 Spread pesto over each thinned turkey steak and lay 2 slices of Parma ham on top of each. Sprinkle the tomatoes and mozzarella evenly over the turkey steaks, then season to taste and roll up each one from the long side.

3 Cut the turkey rolls into 2.5 cm (1 inch) slices. Carefully thread the slices of roll on to 4 metal skewers, dividing them equally among the skewers.

4 Heat the grill on a moderately hot setting. Brush the turkey rolls lightly with oil and grill them for *6 minutes* on each side or until cooked through. Increase or reduce the temperature setting of the grill, if necessary, to ensure that the rolls cook through and brown outside. Garnish with chopped parsley and serve hot, with lemon wedges.

Preparation time: 15 minutes
Cooking time: about 12 minutes
Serves 4

Fish and Shellfish

Fish and shellfish naturally cook quite quickly and combined with a few complementary ingredients, you can create luxurious and delicious meals in a dash.

Seared Scallops with Carrot, Papaya and Red Onion Salad

1 small green papaya or
   1 cucumber
1 carrot, finely shredded
1 red onion, thinly sliced
50 g (2 oz) roasted peanuts
2 tablespoons lime juice

1 tablespoon fish sauce
4 tablespoons finely chopped
   coriander leaves
12 large or king scallops
salt and pepper
chilli oil, to serve (optional)

1 Halve the papaya, scoop out the seeds and then peel the flesh. If using a cucumber, halve it lengthways and scoop out the seeds, then peel it thinly. Finely shred the prepared papaya or cucumber.

2 Mix the papaya or cucumber with the carrot, onion and peanuts. Stir in the lime juice, fish sauce and coriander. Divide this salad among 4 serving plates.

3 Slice the scallops in half horizontally. Heat a large, nonstick frying pan until very hot. Add the scallops and cook them for *1–2 minutes* on each side. Remove the pan from the heat and season the scallops. Arrange the scallops around the salads and serve immediately, offering chilli oil separately for those who may want to spice up the salad.

Preparation time: 15 minutes
Cooking time: 2–4 minutes
Serves 4

Grilled Squid with Coriander Noodles

475 g (15 oz) prepared baby
   squid
basil-flavoured oil, for
   brushing
salt and pepper

1 tablespoon lime juice
2 teaspoons fish sauce
1 tablespoon clear honey
4 tablespoons coarsely
   chopped coriander leaves
2 tablespoons coarsely
   chopped mint
½ red pepper, peeled, cored,
   deseeded and finely diced

CORIANDER NOODLES:
200 g (7 oz) flat rice noodles or
   medium egg noodles
1 tablespoon light soy sauce
   or tamari

1 Cut the squid in half lengthways. Use a sharp knife to score the inner surface of each squid in a criss-cross pattern, taking care not to cut right through. Arrange the scored squid on a grill rack and brush with basil-flavoured oil. Sprinkle with seasoning and set aside.

2 Place the rice noodles in a large bowl and pour in enough boiling water to cover them. Allow to soak for *5 minutes*, then drain and return the noodles to the bowl.

3 In a small bowl, mix the soy sauce or tamari, lime juice, fish sauce, honey, chopped coriander leaves, mint and diced red pepper. Add this mixture to the noodles and toss to mix well.

4 Heat the grill on the hottest setting. Grill the squid for *2–3 minutes* on each side or until just cooked. While the squid is cooking, divide the noodles among 4 plates. Arrange the grilled squid on top of the noodles and serve at once.

Preparation time: 15 minutes, plus soaking
Cooking time: 4–6 minutes
Serves 4

Sesame Prawns with Pak Choi

600 g (1 lb 3 oz) raw tiger prawns, peeled with the tails left on
1 teaspoon sesame oil
2 tablespoons light soy sauce
1 tablespoon honey

1 teaspoon grated fresh root ginger
1 teaspoon crushed garlic
1 tablespoon lemon juice
500 g (1 lb) pak choi
2 tablespoons vegetable oil
salt and pepper

1 Put the prawns in a bowl. Add the sesame oil, soy sauce, honey, ginger, garlic and lemon juice. Season and mix well, then set aside to marinate for *5–10 minutes*.

2 Bring a large saucepan of water to a rolling boil. Cut the heads of pak choi in half lengthways, then blanch them in the boiling water for *40–50 seconds*. Drain well, cover and keep warm.

3 Heat the oil in a large wok or frying pan. Add the prawns with their marinade and stir-fry briskly for *3–4 minutes* or until the prawns are pink and just cooked through.

4 Divide the pak choi among 4 plates, then top with the prawns and any juices from the pan. Serve at once.

Preparation time: 5 minutes, plus marinating
Cooking time: 4–5 minutes
Serves 4

Monkfish Kebabs with Coriander, Chilli and Spring Onion Mash

600 g (1 lb 3 oz) monkfish
  fillet, cut into 2.5 cm
  (1 inch) cubes
125 ml (4 fl oz) natural yogurt
1 teaspoon crushed garlic
1 teaspoon grated fresh root
  ginger
1 teaspoon hot chilli powder
1 tablespoon ground
  coriander
1 tablespoon ground cumin
green salad, to serve
  (optional)

CORIANDER, CHILLI AND
SPRING ONION MASH:
6 large Desirée or King
  Edward potatoes, diced
150 ml (¼ pint) crème fraîche
4 tablespoons finely chopped
  coriander leaves
1 red chilli, deseeded and
  thinly sliced
4 spring onions, thinly sliced
salt and pepper

1 Lay the monkfish in a large, shallow ceramic or glass dish. In a small bowl mix the yogurt, garlic, ginger, chilli powder, ground coriander and cumin. Season the mixture and pour it over the fish. Cover and leave to marinate while you make the mash.

2 Bring a large saucepan of water to the boil. Add the potatoes, bring back to the boil and cook for *10 minutes*, until tender. Drain the potatoes in a colander and return them to the pan.

3 Mash the potatoes and add the crème fraîche. Continue mashing until smooth and then stir in the chopped coriander leaves, sliced chilli and spring onions. Season to taste, cover and set aside.

4 Heat the grill on the hottest setting. Thread the cubes of fish on to 4 metal skewers and cook under the grill for *8–10 minutes*, turning once. Serve immediately, with the mash. A green salad goes well with the monkfish and mash.

Preparation time: 10 minutes
Cooking time: 18–20 minutes
Serves 4

Grilled Mahi Mahi with Mustard and Chive Butter

100 g (3½ oz) butter, softened
2 tablespoons finely snipped
  chives
1 tablespoon prepared English
  mustard
4 portions of mahi mahi or
  halibut (steaks or fillets),
  about 200 g (7 oz) each
4 tablespoons lemon juice
salt and pepper

TO GARNISH:
whole chives
lemon wedges (optional)

TO SERVE:
cherry tomato salad and
  boiled rice or new potatoes

1 In a small bowl, mix the butter, chives and mustard. Turn the butter out on to a piece of clingfilm and press it out into a sausage shape. Wrap the clingfilm around the butter, twist the ends and roll the butter into a neat sausage, then chill it in the freezer for *10–15 minutes* or until firm.

2 Heat the grill on the hottest setting. Lay the mahi mahi or halibut steaks or fillets on a grilling rack and sprinkle the lemon juice over them. Season the fish well and grill it for *6–8 minutes* or until cooked through, when the flesh will flake easily.

3 While the fish is grilling, remove the butter from the freezer and cut it into slices. Transfer the fish to warmed serving plates and top with the butter. Garnish with chives and lemon wedges, if using, and serve at once. A cherry tomato salad and boiled rice or new potatoes go well with the fish.

Preparation time: 5 minutes, plus chilling
Cooking time: 6–8 minutes
Serves 4

Chargrilled Mustard Salmon with Lime Courgettes

4 portions of salmon fillet, about 200 g (7 oz) each
1 tablespoon prepared English mustard
1 teaspoon grated fresh root ginger
1 teaspoon crushed garlic
2 teaspoons clear honey
1 tablespoon light soy sauce or tamari

LIME COURGETTES:
2 tablespoons olive oil
500 g (1 lb) courgettes, thinly sliced lengthways
grated rind and juice of 1 lime
2 tablespoons chopped mint
salt and pepper

1 Place the portions of salmon fillet, skin sides down, in a shallow flameproof dish. The portions should fit snugly in a single layer. Mix the mustard, ginger, garlic, honey and soy sauce or tamari, then spoon this mixture evenly over the fillets. Season to taste and set aside.

2 To prepare the lime courgettes, heat the olive oil in a large nonstick frying pan. Add the courgettes and fry, stirring often, for *5–6 minutes* or until they are lightly browned and tender. Stir in the lime rind and juice, mint and seasoning. Remove from the heat and keep hot.

3 While the courgettes are cooking, heat the grill on the hottest setting. Grill the salmon fillets for *10–15 minutes*, depending on their thickness, until lightly charred on top and cooked through. Serve hot, with the lime courgettes.

Preparation time: 5 minutes
Cooking time: 15–21 minutes
Serves 4

Prawn and Crab Cakes with Chilli Jam

250 g (8 oz) white crab meat
grated rind and juice of 1 lime
4 spring onions, finely
   chopped
1 red chilli, deseeded and
   finely chopped
1 teaspoon grated fresh root
   ginger
1 teaspoon crushed garlic
3 tablespoons chopped
   coriander leaves
3 tablespoons mayonnaise
125 g (4 oz) fresh white
   breadcrumbs

200 g (7 oz) peeled cooked
   tiger prawns, coarsely
   chopped
salt and pepper
oil, for shallow frying
coriander leaves, to garnish
crisp rocket salad or green
   salad, to serve (optional)

CHILLI JAM:
2 red chillies, deseeded and
   finely diced
6 tablespoons sugar
2 tablespoons water

1 Blend the crab meat, lime rind and juice, spring onions, chilli, ginger, garlic, chopped fresh coriander, mayonnaise and breadcrumbs in a food processor until well mixed. Turn the mixture out into a bowl and fold in the prawns with seasoning to taste. Cover and chill while making and cooling the chilli jam. (Alternatively, the ingredients can be mixed by hand.)

2 To make the chilli jam, place all the ingredients in a small saucepan and heat gently until simmering. Cook for *4–5 minutes*, until the sugar has dissolved and the mixture has thickened slightly. Set aside to cool.

3 Divide the prawn mixture into 12 equal-sized portions. Use your hands to roll a portion into a ball, then flatten it into a cake. Repeat with the remaining portions of mixture.

4 Heat the oil in a large nonstick frying pan and fry the cakes for *3–4 minutes* on each side or until golden. Drain on kitchen paper and serve at once, garnished with coriander. Serve the chilli jam spooned over the cakes or separately. A crisp rocket salad or green salad is a good accompaniment.

Preparation time: 15 minutes, plus cooling
Cooking time: 6–8 minutes
Serves 4

Seafood Pilaff

1 tablespoon butter
1 tablespoon vegetable oil
1 onion, finely sliced
1 garlic clove, finely chopped
3 cloves
3 green cardamom pods
1 cinnamon stick
1 dried red chilli
250 g (8 oz) basmati rice
1 teaspoon saffron threads
200 g (7 oz) salmon fillet,
   skinned and cut into 5 cm
   (2 inch) pieces

200 g (7 oz) cod fillet, skinned
   and cut into 5 cm (2 inch)
   pieces
200 g (7 oz) raw tiger prawns,
   peeled
700 ml (24 fl oz) boiling water
salt and pepper
chopped flat leaf parsley, to
   garnish

1 Heat the butter and oil in a large, heavy-based saucepan. Add the onion, garlic, cloves, cardamoms, cinnamon and chilli, and fry, stirring occasionally, for *3–4 minutes*.

2 Add the rice and saffron and cook, stirring, for *1 minute*, then add the salmon, cod and prawns. Pour in the boiling water, add seasoning to taste and bring to the boil. Cover tightly, reduce the heat to low and cook for *10 minutes*.

3 Remove the pan from the heat and leave it to stand, without removing the lid, for *4–5 minutes*. Fluff up the rice with a fork before serving, garnished with chopped flat leaf parsley.

Preparation time: 15 minutes
Cooking time: 14–15 minutes
Serves 4

Trout with Chermoula

Chermoula is a Moroccan spice mixture specifically used for coating or stuffing fish.

8 trout fillets, about
    125 g (4 oz) each

CHERMOULA:
2 teaspoons crushed garlic
1 teaspoon ground cumin
1 tablespoon paprika
½ teaspoon ground
    coriander
2 tablespoons finely chopped
    coriander leaves
2 tablespoons finely chopped
    parsley

2 tablespoons lemon juice
1 tablespoon olive oil
salt and pepper

TO SERVE:
lemon wedges
cucumber salad
warmed ciabatta or
    pitta bread

1 Lay the trout fillets, skin sides down, on the grill rack. Thoroughly mix all the ingredients for the chermoula in a bowl and add seasoning to taste. Spoon the chermoula evenly over the trout. Leave to marinate for *10 minutes*.

2 Heat the grill on the hottest setting. Grill for *5–6 minutes* or until the fish is cooked and its flesh flakes easily.

3 Transfer the fillets and their cooking juices to 4 warmed plates, arranging 2 on each plate. Garnish with lemon slices and serve with a cucumber salad and warmed ciabatta or pitta bread to mop up any remaining chermoula.

Preparation time: 5 minutes, plus marinating
Cooking time: 5–6 minutes
Serves 4

Creamy Prawn Curry

2 tablespoons vegetable oil
1 onion, halved and finely
    sliced
2 garlic cloves, finely sliced
2.5 cm (1 inch) piece of fresh
    root ginger, peeled and
    finely chopped
1 tablespoon ground
    coriander
1 tablespoon ground cumin
½ teaspoon turmeric

200 ml (7 fl oz) coconut milk
125 ml (4 fl oz) vegetable stock
600 g (1 lb 3 oz) raw tiger
    prawns, peeled
grated rind and juice of 1 lime
4 tablespoons finely chopped
    coriander leaves
salt and pepper
boiled basmati or jasmine
    rice, to serve

1 Heat the oil in a large saucepan and fry the onion, garlic and ginger for *4–5 minutes*. Add the ground coriander, cumin and turmeric and stir-fry for a further *1 minute*.

2 Pour in the coconut milk and stock and bring to the boil. Reduce the heat and simmer for *2–3 minutes*. Stir in the prawns, lime rind and juice, then simmer for *3–4 minutes* or until the prawns are pink and cooked through.

3 Stir in the chopped coriander and season the curry well. Serve at once, with basmati or jasmine rice as an accompaniment.

Preparation time: 10 minutes
Cooking time: 10–13 minutes
Serves 4

Desserts

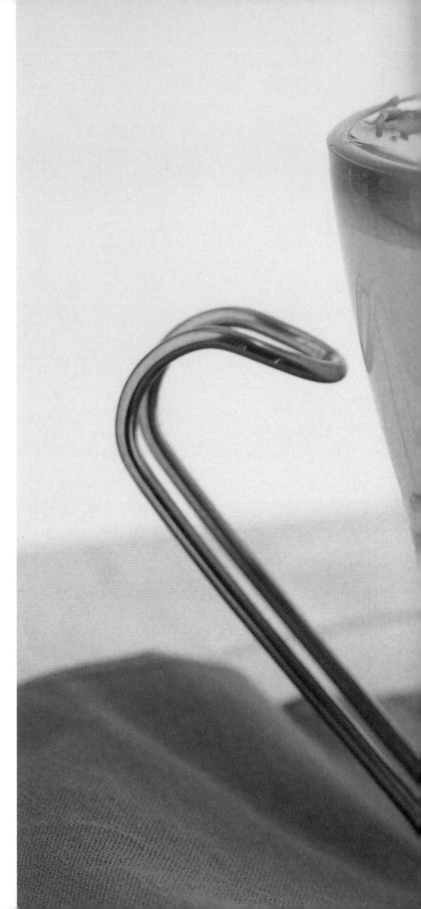

These pretty desserts are not only picture perfect – they taste wonderful as well! Fruits can be combined with irresistable flavours such as mascarpone cheese and chocolate to create a memorable finale to a mid-week meal or special occasion.

Peach and Raspberry Tartlets

These tempting tartlets are simple to make and light to eat. The tartlet cases can be cooked several hours ahead, if necessary, but they should be filled just before they are eaten, otherwise the pastry will soften.

15 g (½ oz) butter, melted
4 filo pastry sheets, each
    about 25 cm (10 inches)
    square
125 ml (4 fl oz) double cream

1 tablespoon soft brown sugar
2 peaches, peeled, halved,
    stoned and diced
50 g (2 oz) raspberries
icing sugar, to dust

1 Grease 4 deep muffin tins with the melted butter. Cut a sheet of filo pastry in half, then across into 4 equal-sized squares. Use these filo squares to line 1 muffin tin, arranging them at slightly different angles and press them down well, tucking the pastry into the tin neatly. Repeat with the remaining pastry.

2 Bake the filo pastry tartlets in a preheated oven, 190°C (375°F), Gas Mark 5, for *8–10 minutes* or until golden. Carefully remove the tartlet cases from the tins and cool on a wire rack.

3 Pour the cream into a bowl and add the sugar, then whip it lightly until it holds its shape. Spoon the cream into the tartlet cases and top with the peaches and raspberries. Dust with icing sugar. Serve at once.

Preparation time: 15 minutes
Cooking time: 8–10 minutes
Serves 4

Cook's Tip
To peel peaches, place them in a bowl and pour in freshly boiling water to cover. Leave for *30–60 seconds*, depending on the ripeness of the fruit (the peel on ripe fruit loosens more quickly). Drain the peaches and slit their peel with the point of a knife, then it will slip off easily.

Tipsy Berry Waffles

A wide variety of fruit tastes excellent pan-fried in butter, with a little sugar and liqueur or brandy. Select ripe, but firm, berries for best results.

15 g (½ oz) butter	1 tablespoon caster sugar
250 g (8 oz) mixed berries, such as blueberries, black-berries and raspberries	2 tablespoons kirsch
	4 tablespoons crème fraîche
	4 waffles

1 Melt the butter in a nonstick frying pan. Add the berries, sugar and kirsch, and cook over a high heat for *1–2 minutes*.

2 Meanwhile, toast or reheat the waffles according to the packet instructions. Spoon the fruit over the waffles and top each portion with 1 tablespoon of crème fraîche. Serve at once.

Preparation time: 5 minutes
Cooking time: 1–2 minutes
Serves 4

Grilled Honey Pears with Minted Mascarpone Cream

Grilling is a great way to cook fruit, either halved or cut into slices, as here. Adding a slightly unusual cream topping transforms the fruit into a special and irresistable treat.

30 g (1 oz) butter	MINTED MASCARPONE CREAM:
2 tablespoons clear honey	1 tablespoon finely chopped mint
4 ripe pears, such as Red William, cored and sliced lengthways	1 tablespoon caster sugar
a little lemon juice	175 g (6 oz) mascarpone cheese
	TO DECORATE:
	icing sugar
	ground cinnamon

1 Melt the butter in a small saucepan. Remove from the heat and stir in the honey.

2 Sprinkle the pear slices with lemon juice as soon as they are prepared to prevent them from discolouring. Line a baking sheet with foil and lay the pear slices on it. Then brush with the butter and honey mixture. Heat the grill on the hottest setting. Grill the pears for *5 minutes*.

3 Meanwhile, make the minted mascarpone cream by lightly whisking the mint and sugar into the mascarpone.

4 To serve, divide the pear slices among 4 plates and add a dollop of the minted mascarpone cream to each portion. Lightly dust with icing sugar and ground cinnamon, and serve at once.

Preparation time: 10 minutes
Cooking time: 5 minutes
Serves 4

Seared Chilli Pineapple

Chilli heat adds a lively edge to the familiar fruity flavour of fresh pineapple. With a hint of anise and a little warm cinnamon, this exotic dessert is good on cool days or hot summer evenings.

25 g (1 oz) butter
1 fresh pineapple, peeled, cored and thickly sliced
1 tablespoon soft brown sugar
2 red chillies, halved lengthways and deseeded, if preferred
1 star anise
ground cinnamon, to dust
crème fraîche, to serve

1 Heat the butter in a large nonstick frying pan. Add the slices of pineapple, sugar, chillies and star anise. Cook the pineapple for about *4 minutes* on each side, until lightly browned.

2 Transfer the pineapple to 4 warmed serving bowls or plates and spoon over the buttery pan juices. The chillies and the star anise can be discarded, if preferred, or arranged on the fruit.

3 Add a dollop of crème fraîche to each portion and dust with a little cinnamon. Serve at once.

Preparation time: 15 minutes
Cooking time: about 8 minutes
Serves 4

Cook's Tip
When you are in a complete rush, remember that you can buy prepared fresh pineapple – then this dessert will be ready in the time it takes to slit a chilli and pan-fry the fruit.

Hot Chocolate Custard with Vanilla Ice Cream

1 tablespoon plain flour
2 tablespoons cocoa powder
200 g (7 oz) sugar
2 egg yolks, beaten
450 ml (¾ pint) milk
1 tablespoon brandy
1 tablespoon chopped walnuts
15 g (½ oz) butter
chopped walnuts, to garnish
vanilla ice cream, to serve

1 Thoroughly mix the flour, cocoa and sugar in a bowl. Add the egg yolks and gradually whisk in the milk until smooth.

2 Pour the mixture into a heavy-based saucepan and cook, whisking continuously, until the custard boils. Reduce the heat to low and cook for *4–5 minutes*, still whisking continuously.

3 Remove the pan from the heat and beat in the brandy, walnuts and butter until well mixed. Pour the custard into serving dishes and decorate with chopped walnuts. Serve at once, with scoops of vanilla ice cream.

Preparation time: 5 minutes
Cooking time: about 8 minutes
Serves 4

Strawberry Fool

Mascarpone cheese is similar to clotted cream in texture. It is unripened, so it does not have a strong 'cheese' flavour, but it resembles a very rich cream cheese.

200 g (7 oz) ripe strawberries, hulled
125 g (4 oz) mascarpone cheese
1 tablespoon finely grated lemon rind, plus extra to decorate
1 tablespoon lemon juice
150 ml (¼ pint) double cream
3 tablespoons caster sugar
redcurrants and blueberries, to decorate

1 Purée the strawberries with the mascarpone and lemon rind and juice in a blender until smooth. Pour the purée into a bowl.

2 Whip the cream and sugar until just stiff, then fold it into the strawberry purée. Spoon the fool into 4 individual bowls or stemmed glasses and chill until ready to serve.

3 Decorate the fool with redcurrants, blueberries and grated lemon rind just before serving.

Preparation time: 10 minutes, plus chilling
Serves 4

Variation
If you have a food processor, frozen raspberries are an excellent ingredient for speedy desserts as they can be processed to an icy powder. Use them in this recipe instead of the strawberries, adding them to the mascarpone after they have been finely processed, then fold in the cream and serve at once. The result is a cross between a fool and an ice cream.

Mango Tarts with Passion Fruit Cream

250 g (8 oz) puff pastry
2 ripe mangoes, peeled, stoned and thinly sliced
25 g (1 oz) butter, melted
100 g (3½ oz) caster sugar
mint sprigs, to decorate

PASSION FRUIT CREAM:
2–3 passion fruit
125 ml (4 fl oz) single cream

1 Line 2 baking sheets with nonstick baking paper. Roll out the pastry to 5 mm (¼ inch) thick and cut out 4 x 12 cm (5 inch) circles. Place the pastry circles on the prepared baking sheets and prick them all over with a fork.

2 Arrange the mango slices on the pastry circles. Spoon the melted butter over the mango slices and pastry, then sprinkle the sugar over the top.

3 Bake the tarts in a preheated oven, 200°C (400°F), Gas Mark 6, for *15–20 minutes* or until pastry is cooked and golden.

4 While the tarts are cooking, cut the passion fruit in half and use a teaspoon to scoop out their pulp into a small bowl. Stir in the cream and mix together.

5 To serve, place the tarts on fairly large individual plates and spoon the cream around them. Decorate with a sprig of mint and serve at once.

Preparation time: 15 minutes
Cooking time: 15–20 minutes
Serves 4

Hot Berry Soufflés

These simple soufflés should be made at the last minute, but the fruit can be puréed in advance. They are superb with high-quality store bought ice cream and the contrast between hot and cold is very refreshing.

15 g (½ oz) butter	**4 large egg whites**
100 g (3½ oz) caster sugar	**icing sugar, to dust**
50 g (2 oz) blackberries	**custard or ice cream, to serve**
200 g (7 oz) raspberries	**(optional)**

1 Use the butter to grease 4 x 200 ml (7 fl oz) ramekins and then coat them evenly with a little of the caster sugar, tipping out the excess sugar. Place the ramekins on a baking sheet.

2 Purée the blackberries and raspberries in a blender or food processor, reserving a few of the berries to decorate, then pour the purée into a bowl. Alternatively, the fruit can be rubbed through a fine sieve to make a smooth purée.

3 Place the egg whites in a large, perfectly clean bowl, then use an electric beater to whisk them until they are stiff, but not dry. Gradually sprinkle in the remaining caster sugar, whisking continuously, and carry on whisking until the whites are stiff and shiny.

4 Gently fold the egg whites into the berry purée, then spoon this mixture into the prepared ramekins. Bake immediately in a preheated oven, 190°C (375°F), Gas Mark 5, for *15 minutes* or until risen and golden.

5 Dust the soufflés with icing sugar and decorate with the reserved berries. Serve immediately. Custard or ice-cream can be served as an accompaniment, if liked.

Preparation time: 10 minutes
Cooking time: 15 minutes
Serves 4

Fig and Honey Pots

It is best to serve this dessert in glass dishes to see the beautiful colours and appreciate the textures of the ingredients.

6 fresh figs, thinly sliced
450 ml (¾ pint) Greek yogurt
4 tablespoons clear honey

2 tablespoons chopped pistachio nuts
2 fresh figs, cut into wedges, to decorate (optional)

1 Arrange the fig slices snugly in the bottom of 4 glasses or glass bowls. Spoon the yogurt over the figs and chill for about *10–15 minutes*.

2 Just before serving, drizzle 1 tablespoon honey over each dessert and sprinkle chopped pistachio nuts on top. Decorate with wedges of fig, if using.

Preparation time: 10 minutes, plus chilling
Serves 4

Tiramisu

1 egg yolk
2 tablespoons caster sugar
1 teaspoon natural vanilla extract
250 g (8 oz) mascarpone cheese
125 ml (4 fl oz) strong black coffee

2 tablespoons brandy
1 tablespoon cocoa powder
16 amaretti biscuits
flake chocolate or cocoa powder, to decorate

1 In a large bowl, beat the egg yolk and sugar until smooth. Stir in the vanilla extract and mascarpone cheese until thoroughly combined, then set aside.

2 Mix the coffee, brandy and cocoa. Break up the amaretti biscuits and stir them into the coffee mixture, then divide half the mixture among 4 bowls or glasses.

3 Spoon half the mascarpone mixture over the biscuit mixture. Then add the remaining biscuit mixture and top with the remaining mascarpone. Dust lightly with cocoa or crumble flake chocolate over the top. Chill before serving.

Preparation time: 15 minutes
Serves 4

Cardamom and Coconut Syllabub with Almond Brittle

Syllabub is so easy and luscious that it is the perfect dessert to share with friends and this subtly spiced version using coconut cream (available from most large supermarkets) is fabulously different from traditional citrus cream.

100 g (3½ oz) sugar
50 g (2 oz) flaked almonds, toasted

SYLLABUB:

200 ml (7 fl oz) coconut cream
300 ml (½ pint) double cream
15 cardamom seeds, lightly crushed
2 tablespoons caster sugar

1 To make the brittle, place the sugar and almonds in a saucepan over a low heat. While the sugar melts, lightly oil a baking sheet. When the sugar has melted and turned golden, pour the mixture on to the baking sheet and set it aside to cool.

2 Pour the coconut cream and double cream into a large bowl. Add the crushed cardamom seeds and caster sugar, then whisk these ingredients together until lightly whipped and just holding soft peaks.

3 Spoon the syllabub into 4 glasses and chill. Meanwhile, lightly crack the brittle into irregular shards. When ready to serve, top the syllabub with some of the brittle and serve the rest separately.

Preparation time: 15 minutes plus chilling
Cooking time: about 10 minutes
Serves 4

Cook's Tip
Cardamom seeds are the tiny brown-black seeds clustered together inside the papery, pale green pods. You will need about 2 green cardamom pods to obtain 15 seeds.

Banana Samosas with Stem Ginger Cream

2 bananas
1 tablespoon soft brown sugar
12 filo pastry sheets, each about 30 x 18 cm (12 x 7 inches)
oil, for deep-frying

STEM GINGER CREAM:

4 pieces of preserved stem ginger, finely diced
2 tablespoons syrup from the ginger
125 ml (4 fl oz) double cream
icing sugar, to dust

1 Coarsely mash the bananas in a bowl and add the sugar. Mix well and set aside.

2 Fold a sheet of filo pastry in half lengthways. Place 2 tablespoons of the banana mixture at one end of the filo, then fold the corner of the pastry over the mixture, covering it in a triangle shape. Fold the triangle of pastry and filling over and over along the length of the filo to make a neat triangular samosa. Moisten the edge with water at the end to seal it in place. Repeat with the remaining filling and sheets of filo pastry.

3 Heat the oil for deep-frying to 180–190°C (350–375°F) or until a cube of bread browns in *30 seconds*. Deep-fry the banana samosas in two or three batches, according to the size of pan, for *3–4 minutes* or until golden brown.

4 Use a slotted spoon to remove the samosas from the pan and place on kitchen paper to drain.

5 To make the stem ginger cream, mix the ginger with the syrup. Lightly whip the cream until it is just firm, then fold in the ginger and syrup.

6 Dust the samosas lightly with icing sugar and serve hot or warm, with the ginger cream.

Preparation time: 20 minutes
Cooking time: 6–12 minutes
Serves 4

Variation
Instead of frying the samosas, place them on a baking tray lined with baking parchment and bake in a preheated oven, 220°C (425°F), Gas Mark 6, for *20 minutes*.

Special Photography:
Neil Mersh
Jacket Photography:
Neil Mersh
Home Economist:
Sunil Vijayakar
Jacket Home Economist:
Sunil Vijayakar